Salt Sugar Spirit
Ellie Ann Deighton

Copyright © 2025 by Ellie Ann Deighton

All rights reserved.

No part of this publication may be reproduced, distributed, or transmitted in any form or by any means, including photocopying, recording, or other electronic or mechanical methods, without the prior written permission of the publisher, except as permitted by Australian copyright law. For permission requests or bulk orders, contact the author.

The story, all names, characters, and incidents portrayed in this production are fictitious. No identification with actual persons (living or deceased), places, buildings, and products is intended or should be inferred.

Book Cover by Ellie Ann Deighton

1st Edition 2025

Contents

Epigraph	1
Ellie's Salt	2
Dedication	4
Foreword	7
1. Innocence.	11
2. Awkwardness.	33
3. Wonderment.	45
4. Oneness.	69
5. Storytime.	85
6. Expansion.	119
The Mystic Lived	125
earth roots sing	131
About the author	133
Author's note	135
Extrasensory: School of Light	137
Acknowledgements	139

Everything is energy. When we recognise ourselves as a part of the natural energy of the world, extrasensory abilities are allowed to flourish. Anything and everything is a possibility. Magic is real. We are the alchemical salt!

Some humans are convinced they are separate from the energy of the world, and anything without a very clear, very logical, very proven definition and explanation is a threat to one's survival and viability. We are addicted to sugar!

We get to choose.

~ evidence suggests

ELLIE'S SALT MANIFEST

FICTION
Ankhara Codes I: An Adventure to Essence
Ankhara Codes II: Allies of the Soul
Ankhara Codes III: A Devotion To Peace

ORACLE CARDS
Fruits of the Feminine

POETRY
'It' is GOLD
Fire Body Warm
Silver Witch Rose
Water River Run
Air Breathes Light

NON-FICTION
Myths of a Mystic Woman

MUSIC ALBUMS
Temple Calling: An Album For Your Altar

ONLINE TRAININGS & COURSES:
Intuitively Me: The Wheel of Life {Air}
Sensual Essence: A Remembering Of Your Bliss {Fire}
The Remembering: Coven Membership {Silver}
Synchronise Me: Emotional Alchemy Training {Water}
Monetise Your Magic: Creative Mastermind {Gold}
Extrasensory: School of Light {Salt}
Permission To Pivot Training {Earth}

more at elliedeighton.com

This is the sixth book of seven in The Elemental Collection; a poetry series focused on the seven essential elements of fulfilment.

You can read The Elemental Collection in any order you choose.

When you saw that out of the corner of your eye?
It was real.
This book is for the part of you that knows it's real,
For the part of you that's afraid of it,
And for the part of you that's ready to lean in.

ELLIE ANN DEIGHTON

Foreword

In my journal I wrote...

June 22 2025

End result: To meet my muse and be informed of the calling of my heart; Salt Sugar Spirit.

I am the magic
And the muse
And I am here
To say to you:

Salt is in the way you breathe
Whether you know it or not
Salt is in what you say to me
And whether your stomach is in knots
Salt is the way you speak to spirit
Or ignore it in the night
Sugar is the way you outsource your power
Pretending you can't receive right

But the truth is your salt
Never went anywhere
You can travel and seek between worlds
The truth is your sugar
Put distraction in the air
And had you lean into mischief and deceptive worlds
You are not alone in your spiritual gifts
You are one of the many like us
You are wise and wonderful, wacky and weird
You'll see clearly if you practice enough
For most believe they either have it or they don't
And they don't like what they have so they hide
Their gifts, separate to the world, believed scary or wrong
Without realising they are magic without trying!
Your salt lifts you up when you're feeling down
Helps remind you that you are connected
Your sugar separates you from the here and now
Helps you wallow in a false disconnection
You'll know the difference, admit it or not
There's nothing secret about it
Your extrasensory gifts are more real than not
Plain and simple, I'll scream and shout it
Because imagine how much easier life could be
If you could receive from your loved ones
If effortlessly you could transcend death's borders

And reach up to discuss your problems
Suddenly it seems all your fears are small
Suddenly there's nothing you can't do
Suddenly you surpass your supposed limitations
Suddenly your consciousness shines through
Suddenly the sugar doesn't have such a grip
Suddenly you are free of the craving
When salt is allowed, you are human, you fully live
And forgetting your soul, is forsaken.

Welcome to Salt.

ELLIE ANN DEIGHTON

Innocence.

She was supported
From the moment she opened her eyes
Seen as magic
Could do no wrong
Until she did
And then she was naughty
And then she became scared
Of getting in trouble
Being told off
Being made out to be bad
Even though she felt in her heart she was good
She couldn't help but fear the rejection
That could come if she told the truth
About what she could see
Right there
As she lay in her sheets
Figures arching over
Terrifying and mean
Standing outside her window
Watching her not sleep
Hovering, making her shiver
Piling pillows around her in heaps
For maybe, just maybe
Tonight they'll come in
Break in through the window
And stab her while she screams
So she smothers herself with pillows
And teddy bears alike

To keep herself safe from the monsters
That are only seen with her eyes
For when she tells her parents
They tell her there's nothing there
There's nothing to be scared of
So why can't she stop being scared?
She looks out of the window
And yes, still there they stand
She doesn't have an angel
To reach out and take her hand
And in fact,
She does
A lot of them, it's true
She just doesn't know it
She doesn't know how to
Call the goddess in
And whisper to the breeze
She doesn't know the trees are friends
Not here to graze her knees
She doesn't know she can use love
That it actually oozes out of her
She only knows when she looks above
There are terrors and they're all around her
– When you can see the salt but it doesn't empower you

In the night
A coldness creeps
Over her body
She pretends she's asleep
She can't help it
Can't make it stop
She's ready to scream
She's cold but she's hot
She keeps her eyes closed
Much too scared to dare them open
She sweats under blankets
For her feet don't need exposing
She hears their breathing
Tries to drown out their moans
But every single night they're there
Creeping her out, she's alone
She goes to her parents
Eventually she can't
She can't take anymore
She has to run she's so scared
So she enters their room
And jumps on their bed
And climbs in between them
Clinging on, she's so scared
Every night they'll hold her
Tell her to go to sleep
They love her, there's no doubt
But they haven't been able to keep

The monsters from the windows
Or the floaties from the room
It's as if they cannot see them
They've shut off their spirit tune
And right when their little one needs them
They fear they've done her wrong
They wish they could receive her
Bring her peace and sing her a song
But they know they can't see what she can
So they hold her and tell her she's with them
And what they don't know is it makes all the difference
But she still wishes they could see them
She still wishes they could tell her what to do
They could help her!
They could help the monsters leave!
But until they open their vision
She's alone in this nightmare of a dream
– If parents had their salt, children wouldn't be afraid of it.

Every single night
She runs away
Because they'll come
Eventually she can't breathe
She closes her eyes
And simply runs
And once again she's in their room
Hoping they can help her
It's the only way she can sleep now
Her room is a storm altogether
She doesn't feel peace
She moves the furniture
Trying to get them out
But one figuration clearly doesn't work
And the next one also lets her down
So she runs into their room
Abandons her own
Wants to sleep in her pile
Dreads being left alone
For sometimes it's so bad
She can't even run
For hours she's stuck and she stares
And nothing can help her
Nothing locks her in
Like the devil in her bedroom yelling at her
– Salt is isolating when you don't understand it

One night
She opens her eyes
And a face appears screaming
Right in front of her
A face of black smoke
An open mouth of skeletal terror
Body freezes
Eyes locked open
Pores leaking a fever
Body stiffens
Teddy squeezed
Might wet the bed
The face screams
And screams
It sounds like a train
So overwhelming she might be deaf after this
And just when the noise peaks
Like the horror in a film
The face moves and flies through her
Like Voldemorte with a broom
Suddenly her whole body rushes with heat
Everything is quiet
But lord forbid she will never fall asleep
She will sit in her chills that night
She will wait and watch
The light turned on
Sitting up
Teddy held to her neck

And wait to see
If that thing is coming back
And if it's ever going to be safe to rest
– Salt is unsettling when you don't know how to listen

It's getting worse
And worse and worse
Which seems impossible
When it started as a terror
What is worse than that?
Why do they call them dreams?
Don't they know she's awake?
This is worse than it seems!
It's being played down
As if she's making it up
But her imagination isn't evil
This can't just be pure dumb luck
She's scared and so is her brother
But not in the same way
He's scared she'll never sleep again
He's scared she's going crazy
Because you see the thing is, he sees them too
He's just magically not afraid
He couldn't care less that they're floating about
He just tells them to go away
He's got things to do
Like snack and sleep
He can't give a penny to distraction
So he tells them, 'Nick off'
And eventually they do
He's handling all the spirit action
But he's the only one
And he's a kid too

And he's not really handling it
His way is suppression too
And the little girl realises
He isn't afraid
So she leans on his protection
Hopes he'll never go away
He likes it for a moment
Big brother acting tough
But soon that's also boring
Losing sleep with her is rough
She keeps coming to his bedroom
Thinking that he'll keep her safe
It's better cause he can see them
So he can tell her the truth, she feels sane
But the real truth neither of them is seeing
Is their guides, right there, needing help
Not fixing or healing or treatment
But listening to, so the kids can walk their path
But they don't listen at all
Their fear leads them astray
Hers in the form of terror, survival,
His trying to keep her safe
And they make a pact
'No more will we see'
And imagine they can turn the Sight off
Close their eyes together
Hold hands and squeeze...
Open wide and it's like the light's on

No more monsters
No more shadows of black
They haven't solved the problem
But they certainly found a hack
The Sight is now in boxes
Trapped inside both their hearts
They'll come back to it later with focus
And embrace this as their family art.
– Salty kids are resilient as fuck

What if they didn't turn it off?
Would their lives be different?
More amazing?
Or more traumatic?
Would they know a different type of love sooner?
Would they have cracked the code?
The trouble is
We can only imagine
And really
We'll never know
– The only thing we know is that their salt was there all along

'Mum,

I've always seen you as golden

And I don't mean perfect

I mean really golden

Like somehow when you walk there's an orb about you

And I can see them

The shadows

They bounce off you

They don't touch

I wonder if it's saved your life

And actually,

I wonder how many times it's saved your life

And I know for sure

It saved mine.'

– A mother's love is its own special salt

'Dad,
I don't know if you know
But I saw you floating
And I didn't know what was going on
I don't know how old I was
I think I put it down to imagination
But I saw it
I walked in the room
You were meditating
Laying down
On your back
I wasn't meant to be there
You told me later the depth of your practice freaked you out
I would have freaked out too if I realised I was flying.'
– Salt untapped explains a lot

I'm imagining there was a world
Where grandparents knew their salt
Because their grandparents did
And so they taught their children
And they consulted their grandchildren
And the wisdom was passed
The love
The light
The evoking of such magic
The dancing of such connection
The bliss of such revelation
And I think maybe that's where we've been
And I know in my heart it's where I'm going
– Salt is like air in the future, simply part of being human

If salt was part of being human,
Happened like breathing,
Connected us like a bonfire,
Cleansed us like the water,
Was gifted to us in our gold,
Came to us in the silver thread,
Was of our body as we are of the earth,
Nothing would be different to how we are right now
– Salt is part of being human

Sugar and salt are very different
I'm talking about the salt of the earth
The salt in the sea
The salt in your body that you need to breathe
And the sugar that is made
The sugar that disconnects
The sugar that distracts
Is the television series really supporting your true path?
Or is it switching yourself off to who you truly are?
– You know your sugar, you know your salt

To be extrasensory
Is to use our extra senses
Not extra special
Not extra for some
Extra because they've been switched off and forgotten
Not because we can't
Not because it's not available to us
Not because it's hard
Not because it's cool
Just because we are human
Just because we are connected
Not because we are mad
Because we are love
Because we are one

So surely
Obviously
Anything is possible
And certainly
Obviously
A spirit realm isn't outrageous
Nor a dragon
Or a fae
Or a pristine elf
So let's just imagine for a moment
We all have salt
And maybe we can start sprinkling our tables with it
– Salt isn't just a dressing, it's part of the meal

I'm not saying there can't be good sugar,
I love fruit
Our brains need it
But play with me
Be less logical
More symbolic
Lean into the vibe with me
Salt holds the boundaries of your truth
Sugar collapses you
– You know your sugar, you know your salt

You can see it in other people
The sugar
And the salt
You can see which they pour over their table
Which one is filling their heart
You can see in their health, in their body
Does the energy purely flow?
Are they stuck and trapped in their physique?
Have they forgotten the soul they know?
You can see it in the way they share
They're vulnerable or tight
For those one with their power
Have nothing to lose in a fight
They've nothing to protect for they are whole
But sugar pokes holes in an instant
They lose perspective on what they love
They find they are living a projection
Now they're fantasising rather than dreaming
And yes there is a difference
The fantasy connects to false highways
And the dreams are what your soul wants to be living
– Sugar and salt are palpable choices

Awkwardness.

Sugar is what happens
When we forget the salt
And it turns to crust
And our system is a bit fried
We're uncomfortable with life
We're in denial of death
We can't imagine that we're imagining everything
It seems bad to make it up
We're overweight and unhealthy
We are terrified of ourselves
Our power is pocketed
– You are salt, you don't need fake sugar

Imagine the awkwardness
Of realising your children are your teachers
And you already knew that
But somewhere along your journey you had forgotten
And forgotten that spirituality could be part of that
They aren't just teaching you patience
Kindness
Softness
Presence
Play
They are teaching you to collapse your separation from all of time and space
Take it in
They are teaching you to collapse your separation from all of time and space
The timelines are collapsing
You can have it now
The magic
The memory
The mesmerising life
Or you can have it now
The mundane
The mundane
The mundane
– Salt is naturally in all of us, but oh, how the children and the elders remember

I ask my nan
What she feels will come to her in death
I don't know
She says
But I hope
She says
And I'll keep her hopes a secret
But I won't keep it a secret that I am convinced
All her hopes will come true
And I'll see her when she's there
– Salt is eternal

Imagine my surprise

After all the terror

The first time I was told I had a gift

To not be afraid of it

To cherish it

To lean into it

To share it for the greater good

To be one with it

To master it

To enjoy it

Umm, excuse me, did you say enjoy it?

You must not have been listening.

This has been my terror

My fear

My limitation

My childhood trauma

This is the reason I am afraid of the night

Much more scary than men or humans

There is no enjoying this

And then I took a moment to soak in their eyes

To look around the room

Thirty souls

Looking at me expectantly

Receiving me at my word

Receiving me in my gifts

Envious even

Curious for sure

Asking questions

Wanting to know more
Wishing to tap in for themselves
Hoping to see into their future
And I softened
An awkwardness dropped off me
It fell
I fell
As if the fake, scared self didn't have to cling here anymore
And then I was just seeing
'Nine,' I said.
'There are nine of them here for the ritual.'
She smiled, my teacher,
And we went on
Acknowledging them
Including them
United with them
And suddenly
Clairvoyance wasn't so bad
– Salt comes in many different forms, mine came with a vision

I wanted to die
Awkward!
Young, vibrant, clever, fit, healthy, full of life
And I didn't want to be here!
Picture this:
People all over the world in the wellness fight
Struggling to maintain their position here on earth
And I am wilting by choice
I do not want this
I am sick and tired of it
And I am in the car
Alone
A friend driving behind me
I don't have far to go
A couple of streets
Two turns of the wheels and I'll be home
And I feel it
The shadow comes in and the car goes cold
The selenite on my dashboard turns black
I am empty, suddenly a shell of a human
A shell filled with terror
Later I'll find out my friend saw the 'thing' enter the vehicle
She panicked too
She watched the moment it lay its hand on me
If that's what we can call it
Perhaps more a claw
Perhaps more... bones
And I collapsed into it

I wanted it to be over

So I said yes

It came in

She saw it and she feared what would happen next

But for a few blissful moments I didn't fear life at all

I was simply ready to end it

It entered my body

And the world became black and white

And suddenly a simple choice to not be here anymore

Felt so easy

And so pure

And I swerved into the beauty of a tree at full pace

And something else swept into me

Scooped it out

Maybe it was Jesus

Maybe a guardian angel

An ancestor

The goddess

I'll never know and I need not

But the 'thing' was gone

And my vision coloured again

Awkward…

I had tried to die

I had been ready to end this life on my mother's street

But I didn't

The colour returned

I went home

I panted, cried, screamed inside

Sat in my mother's golden aura
She couldn't see the way the shadow creatures bounced off her
I couldn't breathe away from her
But I was breathing
And on that day, that was the point
– Before the salt became clear

Before the salt became clear
Which took quite a time
I was awkward at being myself
Uncomfortable in my own skin
Trying to explain away who I was
Pretending I wasn't receiving what I was experiencing
Switching it off
Switching me off
Spilling over
Uncontrollable
Afraid of my power and confident of my mind
Cleverness was a value
– But then the salt became clear and all I valued was soul

The salt became clear
And years of effort
Years of focus
Dreams of medicine
Of surgery
Of excelling in academia
Dissolved
I left
Everything changed
No one knew what was going on
Least of all me
But I had seen the soul
I had seen the salt for what it was
And there was no going back
– Seeing the salt will set you free

ELLIE ANN DEIGHTON

Wonderment.

When I met Love
I thought it was an instrument
Something to attain
A spirit to capture
An achievement to lock in
And I was wrong
Deeply wrong
Because I found Love was a spirit
Shared between two people
Chosen between few people
And that not everyone was dancing in love
Not everyone was committed to truth
They were committed to validation
Or a zest for punishment in the lack of validation
And I found in meditation
I was mapping bodies
I was seeing spirits

And very legitimately
This is how I avoided STIs!
Because I could see it in the field
And I would say no to it
I would warn my friends
And they'd still go home with it...
They'd learn in the end
You follow the spirit
You allow yourself to see the spirit
And Love,
The real Love
Presents itself
Which absolutely wasn't what I expected of my spiritual journey
But in hindsight
That pleasurable thing...
I can't fathom that I expected anything else
– More salt, more love

Sugar is the craving, the false light, the quick fix
The 'doesn't work'
'Wasn't good enough'
'Didn't have it in me'
'Over too quickly'
'Gimme another one, that wasn't it'
Eat until I feel like shit
Fuck until it's 'out' of my system
No
Move until I can move no more
No
Shuffle around my feelings
No
Binge and hope and pray
– Salt is the spirit you really need for it is the spirit you are

When I write
And move and exercise
And make music
There is a movement of my spirit that happens
I have learnt to surrender to the muse
And in some ways it comes so naturally
Writing music to me is as easy as deciding I'm going to feel
Feel
And then there is a tune to it
And then there are lyrics
And the song is free of any cage created in the land of ideas
It's here now
Maximum fifteen minutes later
That would be a stretchy, sticky one!
In writing
I've also always felt that
A feeling
A tiny thread to pull
And away I go
Thousands of words and poems and stories later
Eventually the thread will end or change colour
But I used to not be able to navigate it very well
It used to be spontaneous
And now
I have learnt
In wonderment with my spirit
That it's always there
I used to stress

If I got interrupted
NO I CAN'T ANSWER THE DOOR I'M WRITING
AND IF I DON'T WRITE IT RIGHT NOW IT'S GONE FOREVER
AND IT WILL BE YOUR FAULT
AND I WILL TAKE IT OUT ON YOU
It made me angry
Because I couldn't see I was the one with the power
Even though I was
Now I know
I am the one with the spirit
So it doesn't matter
Interrupt me all you like
This story will be told
The poem will come out
You'd best believe
(But I don't care if you do)
That I will write regardless of excuse
I have learnt the difference between fucking around
Distractions that don't matter
And allowing the flow of life to move through me
Knowing that the book will be taken care of
Now you may not be a writer
(Though I think we all are storytellers)
But you do have a spirit
A flow
A salt in you that doesn't change
I will always be a writer, a singer, a poet, a teacher, a musician

This is in my sacred pulse as a being
This connects me to my spirit
This plugs me into a greater truth
And through all my seasons it doesn't change
There are songs for winter, summer, autumn, spring
Poems for childhood, teenage years, adulthood and eldership
Teachings for maiden, mother, crone
Books for e v e r y t h i n g
There will always be these parts of me
And now I know the way to see through the dust
The way to clear the blur
Is to connect to spirit
To sprinkle salt on myself
And listen to my truth
And write
– Salt is a muse for your soul too

ELLIE ANN DEIGHTON

It is a wonder to me
That we hold these stories
Not in our minds
But in our imaginations
So we really aren't holding anything
We really are rogue
Not rogue as in dishonest
Rogue as in *wild*
It is *wild* to me, the limitless expanse of possibilities
Between our legs
Inside our chests
In our third eyes…
Wow
We are incredible beings
And yet

We tell ourselves we'll believe it when we see it
Then decide we didn't see it, we imagined it
Then decide the imagination is a childish thing,
Then decide children have no credibility when it comes to wisdom,
Then switch off the connection to magic
And wonder where it all went wrong
Wonder why we are fixated on paying bills on our way to dying
Rather than focused on freely living as who we truly are underneath the flesh
And including, honouring, revering the flesh that lets us have this life experience
Why?
Well
The answer is in our imagination
– Who cares if you imagine your salt? Let's care if your imagination opens or closes the real salty you

You are salty

When you sing

When you make love with an open heart

And when you close your heart to the world

You are salty

Whether you are happy, spiritual, open, obsessed with magic,

Living your true nature and purpose

Serving others and being a really fabulous person

Or

Burdened by life itself,

Wishing you weren't here,

Missing the point,

Not seeing the relevance of it all,

Stuck down the toilet

Yup

You are still salty

The salt is still there

It's just some of you

(Sometimes myself included)

Have crusted the salt with sugar

Distracted yourself from the realness of the love you are

Told yourself it must look and feel a certain way

So cut yourself off from the magic of yes and both and this is *way* better

You've told yourself ignorance is sweet

But this sugar is eating away at you

Protecting you only from the shock horror of being yourself

Which actually is a great, deep sense of peace

Being yourself
A friend said to me today on my podcast
She used to hustle in business and force and push
And now she knows
What is for her will come
It may not be what she thinks
But it will be better
It will be true
And she will recognise it when she sees it
And then
She relaxes to receive
She knows the goods are coming
So business is a delight to her
Always a surprise
And such is this life if you let it be
– Sugar doesn't actually sweeten your salt, it buries it

The first time I had sex and
Focused on the heart being open
The heart in my body
And the heart in front of me
And the heart of the spirit between us
The world opened
My body opened in ways I couldn't explain or believe
And suddenly I realised
That the open heart lets out the spirit
Sprays salt everywhere
As if it is a sacred water blessing everything it touches
This salt can be a liquid,
Shapeless
Inexplicable
Holy
And when the body of my lover filled with love from his heart
And my body filled with love from my heart
And we overflowed into each other
Suddenly the world was beyond what we'd ever known
Suddenly the walls between us dissolved
Suddenly the alignment of our paths became obvious
Suddenly we were in love
Quicker than 'normal'
Not how it was meant to be
Defying barriers dressed up as good boundaries
The limitations snapped
And we found ourselves
Stepped out of our temple in our wholeness

Feeling more like ourselves
Not enmeshed
Not needing one another
Relishing
Delighting
Devoting
Triggering and leaning in
Receiving
Salt isn't about creating separation
Like we see in witches circles keeping things in or out
It's about clarity, about spirit, about intention
And it shows us what is ours to choose
– Salt helps us choose the love that is right for us (and what's right for me may not be right for you)

For a long time I wondered
What is my sexuality?
This movement of spirit inside me
That wants to explode into stars
And be shared with multiple types of people?
I couldn't fathom choosing
I couldn't fathom the limitation
I could not describe my type
I have dated
Women
Men
Bald
Long hair
Short hair
Dreadlocks
Blonde
Silver
Brown
Black
Tall
Short
Slim
Buff
Hairy
Smooth
My age
Younger
Older

Blue eyes
Green eyes
Brown eyes
Grey eyes
Hazel
Australian
American
African
Mauritian
French
Canadian
English
And none of them could be described as similar people
But oh, I loved their souls
It was their salt I fell for
It was the sugar that ruined us
But those of us on the path of salt still have love
Still love each other even if it looks different
Still care for each other even if the intimacy is changed
And I remember a teacher saying to me
It matters not what they look like
And everything that their spirit speaks to you
And the dates that went nowhere for me
Were the dates where the soul was caged and I never got to meet that person
For every person I really meet
Oh, how I love them
– Salt is limitless, boundless, everlasting, beyond the body, real

ELLIE ANN DEIGHTON

This book isn't about sex
It's about salt
But you see
Salt is everything you are
And we all came from love
So it makes sense it gets a feature
– Salt isn't sex, but it includes it

This book isn't about writing either,
But it's part of my salt
Calling itself forth
Begging gently to be expressed
The calling of salt never goes away
– If your salt says to write, who are you to say no?

I see so many say no to their salt

Tell themselves and me they aren't ready

Tell me it's not possible

Tell themselves they aren't going to make it

And I think to myself (or yell to them)

Do you really think you have this dream in you just to imagine it?

Do you really think your dreams are fake?

Do you really think your spirit came to earth to receive none of what it wants?

Okay

– ~~Who are you to choose your salt~~ Who are you to *not* choose your salt?

I wonder

About a reality

A place

A world

Where we all live by the salt in our seams

Sew a new reality together

Generously and melodically thrive in our village

Your salt helps

My salt helps

All our salt is needed and complementary

And then I think

What the fuck are we doing?

– More salt, please

Imagine a pilgrimage
Being a life well-led from the salt
Simply covering the distance of our callings
Leaving the rest for the rest
Don't get involved in politics if your calling is art
Don't make art about horses if your calling is political
DO YOU
That's the life pilgrimage salt invites us on
– Are you on the salt path?

I'm curious

Not judging

Just wondering

Why would you want to be anything other than yourself?

– Salt is where you are, where the real you lives

Witch's salt
Is what it's called
When one rubs salt into the mix with the ashes of rituals past
Burnt leaves
Burnt paper
It could be anything apparently
According to Wikipedia
Which you know is one hundred percent accurate
And now the salt is black
And has extra magical powers
But the only thing that gives salt its power is salt being itself
– You are like salt

You are a wonder

An anomaly

A miracle to even exist

A special, very special individual

Just like the rest of us

Exactly the same as your neighbour

Completely reflected in your beloveds' eyes

Doing your best just like I am

– How could your salt ever be an accident or an ailment?

ELLIE ANN DEIGHTON

Oneness.

Salt was an ailment when I couldn't be myself.
– Salt wasn't the problem

Business was hard when I ignored the salt
— Salt was what was missing

Death is hard when I disconnect from the salt
– Salt is a bridge between worlds

Spirituality is shameful when I neglect the salt in myself
– Salt is not what's embarrassing, forgetting to be myself is

ELLIE ANN DEIGHTON

Forgetting is part of the path of salt
– Salt isn't looking for perfection, only truth

Maybe you can let your salt speak one layer at a time
– Salt isn't rushing you

ELLIE ANN DEIGHTON

You can feel the calling of the salt
– Salt isn't separate to you

Your fear of the salt is what is making salt scary
— You can learn to love the salt

Appreciating the salt is what transforms the scary into the healing
– True salt promotes oneness

When you are whole, you see the salt
– And when we all hurt, we look for the salt as if it's the only real thing in existence

ELLIE ANN DEIGHTON

There are a million ways to tread salt paths
– Not all salt is the same but all salt is salt

You are salt at your essence
— Are we getting salt yet?

Perhaps it is time for a salty story
About a little girl
Who wanted to see her grandpa one last time
She felt bad when she realised what death meant
And she had laughed when she found out he was dead
The salt had stirred a joy in her
You see, her grandpa was suffering
And she was just a little girl
So she didn't know
But she *knew*
So when she heard the good news
He isn't suffering anymore
She laughed for his freedom
Then retracted in shame of her own freedom
Everything seemed misunderstood
She never saw him again in the flesh
She never went to his funeral
She grew to be a woman not knowing where or if he was buried or burned
But every time she walked to the pond she saw him

He was sitting there every time
She could talk to him
Glance in awe at him in his glow
And every time she saw those giant red flowers
She saw him
And when she reflects on Christmas,
Sometimes she sees him
Occasionally in adulthood he sends her messages
Gentle
Soft
A beckoning from the otherworld
She knows it's tied to this world
She still doesn't know what death means
But salt showed her it doesn't mean the end
– Salt is just the beginning

Storytime.

I'm inspired
By the stories and the eagerness of my best friend
Who always wanted another bedtime story
Didn't care for the nature of the story
Only for its saltiness
– You can thank Paige for this chapter of salt stories

I met someone
And he threw me for six
I wasn't ready
Wasn't expecting him
He was in the flesh
I wasn't looking for someone
But there he was
And I didn't know the answer
I was in the living room crying
Why am I feeling like this?
I shouldn't be feeling like this!
And then appeared
Two familiar ancestors
And one lifted me up
Danced with me
A gentle waltz
Whispered to me
A gentle nod
His song came on the Spotify rotation
One out of many thousands
Already on shuffle
And then he was gone
As quickly as he came
He only had a short message
But he brought me peace
Integrity
Clarity
Truth

Calm

And then there was another

She was standing there patiently

She'd been watching us waltz

And then

She smiled

She sung

She told me,

'Everything is okay dear,'

And it's all I needed to hear

And she was gone too

And that was months ago

And everything really has been okay

– Salt knew the truth

I wasn't always 'together' in my clairvoyance
I used to get drunk
Simulate some confidence
Because when I was sober
It all just felt like insanity
But when I was drunk
I didn't even care if was my imagination
I loved it
And to be honest
I could tell it wasn't my imagination
I could feel them
Hear them
See them
Speak to them
And it was easy
But sometimes
I took the drink too far
And one time
I was in the shower
Trying not to vomit
Knowing that a vomit might make myself feel better
But not while I was in the shower!
No thank you
Please, no thank you
And right then
While I was kneeling at the bottom of the shower
Unsure of the pending chunder
A man appeared

I groaned
Really?
Now?
Come on
I could hardly believe it
But I should have known
This house always had them
(a symptom of a friend who's more gifted than she realises)
Anyway
It's a giving thing to communicate with the dead
To liaise their last wishes
To find their relatives
To hear them out
To open the veil for them to go home to peace or whatever is next
And I didn't have anything to give
But I did promise him
'Another time, come back'
He frowned
Wasn't very impressed
And to be fair
I wasn't being very impressive
It was the middle of the day after all!
Anyway
He came back
And when he came back
It was with a vengeance
– When you treat salt irreverently, you might get slapped

He came back
Unexpectedly
That's how that works
I didn't see it coming
Time had passed
I'd all but forgotten about him
I was really still learning, you see
I wasn't quite confident to call to him
I thought I might receive somebody who wasn't him
So I did nothing
And there were consequences
Phone calls from a friend late at night
She'd been woken up strangled
Over and over again
Crying, she called
I came to her house
There he was
And he was angry
And there was a little girl
She was terrified
She was crying in the corner
And I don't know the stories they tell me…
How real they are
How true
How dramatised in their deaths they become
But his story shook me
His story involved his mum
His mum was the reason he died

And it was terrible
Intentional
Traumatic
Horrible to witness
And he was taking this terror out on my friend
As if she was his mum
As if she would pay for this other woman
He wouldn't listen
He couldn't see she wasn't his mother
So I called in The Mother
Mother Mary
Now I'm not religious
Never have been
But I do believe in the Holy Spirit
I have met Jesus
And Mother Mary would tend to me when I was wrapped in fear
So,
Often
So when I needed help with a spirit
Something I couldn't slice through
Something beyond me,
I would humble myself
Let it be beyond me
And call a friend.
She was the friend
First she came in and wrapped her arms around my friend
I asked her if she could feel it
She said yes

I waited
She relaxed
The space dissipated a little bit
Lighter and easier
He was still angry and he wasn't listening
So I called in more love
Mary Magdalene
Will you hold this man in his pain?
She nodded and smiled
She's really good at that, you see
No demons scare her for she is living in love and wow
It didn't take long for him to shift
He melted in her arms
Cried and cried and cried
Hours I waited
Witnessed
As my friend cried and calmed in Mother Mary's arms
And this man, I called him Max, cried in Mary Magdalene's arms
All the while the little girl wept in the corner
She didn't want anyone
She only wanted Max gone
So she waited and watched with me
We both became the witnesses to the Mary alchemy
Max softened, apologised and went to the light
Magdalene nodded to me and left
My friend visibly changed as soon as he walked out and through
She opened her eyes and looked at me
'Is it over?'

'For him it is,
But we still have a little girl to tend to.'
She was snuffling now
But much at ease with Max's disappearance
I sat on the floor in the corner with her
Mother Mary still present
And she looked up at me
'Can you help me find my grandpa?'
I broke a little bit
Choked up
I'd never dealt with a child like this before
Not one so scared and innocent
And I'd never found someone on the other side
But I wanted to
So I did
I decided if I opened the veil, he would be there
So I opened the veil,
And there he was
Surrounded by light
He held out his arms
And her eyes opened wide with delight
And she ran to him
They embraced
He nodded to me
He shed a tear
And they went into the light
So I closed up the zipper I had opened
Ask Mother Mary to tend to the room

She paused for a moment
'You've done well, child'
She smiled and left
Now it's just me and my tear-stained friend
We're exhausted
It's been hours
Very late at night
But the energy is clear
She'll sleep well now
And I've just had the most beautiful experience of my life
– On the other side of the fear, salt is the most beautiful gift imaginable

I don't remember
Meeting the Marys
Isn't that a funny thing?
Isn't that something you'd think I would remember?
But I don't
I do remember them being there
Over and over
Once I'd discovered their existence
In adulthood, mind you
After a lot of fear
I began to find the light in my gifts too
I began to see my guardian angels
I began to see fairies and wishes
I began to see beyond the fear
And somewhere
In seeing beyond the fear
I met the most powerful women as guides
And to this day
They continue to change my life
– Salt isn't something you graduate from

I am forever a student to my salt
I remember Mum's friend being very, very ill
I hadn't known her
But I'd felt the pain in Mum's pending loss of her
And I was laying in bed
Eyes closed
And I felt something
Opened my eyes
There she was standing at the end of my bed
I didn't know what she looked like but I knew
'It's over now,'
Was all she said
And I knew I had to tell my mum
So I got up and spoke to her
She cried
Rang for confirmation
Her friend was dead
But there was a special sense of peace that she had come
She'd known she could come to me
That I would pass her message on
So I did
All in the space of five minutes
All in the face of someone I'd never known
– Sometimes salt is as simple as that

I ran an event

In my early days of event hosting

It was a sister circle

A dance of sorts

We played music and sung and shared

It was beautiful

And then we took photos of the group in the mirror

And we had company in the picture

It was beautiful

The white skirts of a dancer

She was with us

It felt peaceful

It didn't feel like anything was wrong

The energy was calm in the studio

However

As soon as one stepped out into the hall

Which was necessary for toilets

Necessary for lighting

Necessary to lock up

A different energy landed

A creepy chill that ran neck to fingertip

It wasn't welcoming

It certainly wasn't beautiful

I wanted out

We wanted out

But we had to go that way to lock the door and turn out the lights

So reluctantly

Off we went

And before I knew it
A creature on the stairs
Descending right to us
I could see, my friend could feel
We filled with terror
This horror too real
We ran for the entrance
Shutting the door
We're still in the hallway
Now it's spirits galore
Surrounded by shadows
Can't see a way out
The creature descended
Throats froze, couldn't shout
The panic was consuming
I didn't know what to do
My friend was now crying
Grief and terror all we knew
I LOVE YOU
I screamed
I don't know how it happened
A need to scream came over me
I don't know how it happened
Still in shock we looked at each other
Because all the shadows froze
As if in shock in their own way too
We couldn't care, we had to go
I tapped her shoulder,

It made her move
We started to run
Had nothing to prove
We just wanted out
Speedily locked the door
Ran into the car park
Accelerators hit the floor
Straight to my brother's house
We parked and breathed and panicked
Thank God that is over
I thought, I'll never again plan it
I could have quit circles
Quit magic on the spot
But that night magic saved me
Believe it or not
That same night my mother held me
Protected me with her gold
Reminded me of the witches
Of the power of stories of old
And in the midst of all the terror
I decided I would not quit, not this Queen
I realised this gift was just untamed
And I could learn to manage what I'd seen
I didn't know where to start
But intended I'd figure it out
And I'd like to tell that version of me she did it!
She got through all mountains of doubt
She created a life filled with magic

And yes, true time it would take
But everything else left her life
For with magic, there's no space for fake
And really it opened the floodgates
Her furs fell, she'd howl at the moon
And women, men and children would follow her
Unlocking their magic too
You'd never have guessed such fear dwelled here
Between her ribs, her legs, her ears
But it just goes to show, little creatures
We can all live beyond all our fears
– Salt raises us into our purpose but we have to raise ourselves above the fears

You see, salt may have been frightening once
And it still challenges me sometimes
But salt is how I live
Magic is how I write my books
I speak to a guide who channels through me
My songs are a spirit I can't hold back
My teachings are like a possession
When I make love I dissolve
When I work on someone's body I see the unimaginable
When I travel I plan nothing
Everything is led by the salt
Everything is a calling
Everything is intangible
Until it is completely tangible
Because eventually
Even the most bizarre calling makes sense
All relationships resolve themselves
All trips reveal their true purpose
Everything comes together
Eventually
Everything comes together
And that's it.
– You either follow salt or you don't, but either way you know it's right there

I have so many stories
And they aren't all mine
Some are so sacred
Moments in time
When spirits left bodies
When relatives died
When friends have their friends go
Crossing through suicide
There's always been a phone call
A friend who needs some help
And I do what I can
But those stories I don't need to tell
The point is we have the power
To communicate more than we know
And it doesn't always make sense
I've been scared more than I've shown
But always in the aftermath
I am filled with such a love
That nothing else can matter
I can tell these gifts are from above
It's not that I'm more special than you
More connected or more able
I've just been so willing to sit in my fear
That magic now lives at my table
So if you do want to
Lean into your gifts
Regardless of your life so far
Know that you can do this

But you will face yourself
Resistance is true
You'll have to decide to rise above
And let connection win through
But if you are willing to go the distance
And feel you will follow the call
You know where I am, for real, for assistance
It's what The Remembering is for
It's my magical hub
Where you can share your journey
You won't be alone
And you'll receive a natural learning
Rituals and seasons and spells and witches
And you'll come together, receiving your gifts
And if you want *more*,
If you want deeper than shares,
You can become my student
I can meet you there
In the part of you that fears your opening
I will shine a light
To the part of you so willing and hoping
Your ego will put up a fight
So The Remembering is there
For the magic of your heart
To become a way of your life
Extrasensory School is waiting
For your magical purpose
To be trained to your delight

Two layers, two levels, two different modes
Both magic, both special, both princes to toads
There's no right or wrong way, when ritual is to be lived
But your results tell the real story, is what you're doing effective?
I'm not having a go,
I just want you to be honest,
Because I want you to have your most magical life
And so many of us define our gifts as horrors
– Your salt is fucking magical and sometimes you need help with it

Late at night
Friends sit in a circle
By candlelight
Chatting up a whirlpool
The candle explodes
Red wax on the wall
One woman panics
Growing wings she's so tall
I tell her I see them
She starts to relax
She feels really seen then
Has questions to ask
'They are your spirit'
I tell her with glee
'Whenever you need them
Close your eyes and breathe'
From that day she did
She was a little less scared
From friends sitting in a circle
To a lady, wings wide spread
– Salt will have you lift each other up because you'll see we're all connected

The selenite that changed colour
Was a sickening thing
It took days for it to turn back
Like my car's aura had to grieve
But when it went clear
The relief was immense
An external symbol
There was nothing left to fear
Until the next time
It started to go dark
But this time was different
Like a walk in the park
Compared to the terror
Of the first time it changed
The second time was easy
Wow, I was so brave
It's like the one time was enough
To show me I could do it
Yes, to live through that was tough
But wow, did I get through it!
Three days it took to leave the house
Three days it took to rise
But the rest of my life has been easier since
And that is the biggest prize
  – Lean into your salt with love and you'll find the gold

I was sat with a mother,
Not mine but a friend's
And she told me my guide was there
I didn't understand
You see, I hadn't met them yet
I wasn't sure they were real
But here they were offering support
I lean in, through the fear I feel
I take her hands
Her face changes shape
And through her eyes I see
The mystic picture of my guides
My ancestors
The lion family
And I cannot understand how I am seeing
And if what I am seeing is real
I drop her hands
Lean back for a moment
And the lion face completely disappears
What did you see?
My friend's mother asked
But I do not have the words
Shall we try again?
She leans in with a smile
And I figure it can't get any worse
So I lean in
I take her hands
I let her show me what's golden

And instead of snow I see tropical lands
Confusing for my life in that moment,
She said this was the future,
I didn't understand,
I am utterly convinced she is wrong
And then I am broken
I can't fight it anymore
I tell her
We'll see when this is over
She gestures to my ankle
It's injured and I'm hobbling
Prove to yourself you are a healer
I'm confused,
Considering leaving medicine
And wondering if surgeons are such feelers
She shakes her head
Shows me other ways to heal
Sparks fly down my leg
And I refuse to feel
The pain that has been there
Aching for days
Stopping me from walking
Interrupting my ways
Then I fall asleep
Not sure what happened next
But in the morning I wake
And I'm dancing on my legs
And then I realise

Hang on, my ankle is broken
But right before my eyes
The bruising gone, the swelling broken,
My ankle is fine!
I tell my friend's mum
She smiles the whole time
Says magic is truly fun
And something in me shifts
There are different ways to heal!
And cutting isn't always it
I'm really starting to feel
I walk and run and jump and skip
And yep, my ankle is fine
So after all the winter planning
That tropical horizon was mine
– Salt broke what I thought was possible and put me on the warmer track of life

I felt my guides put their hands on my back
And first, I coiled in fear
Then I felt them for real, not reflex,
And everything comforting felt near
I surrendered to the comfort
To the familiar in what I could feel
And wisdom flooded into me
And magic became real
– Salt allows your connection to all of time and space

ELLIE ANN DEIGHTON

I can feel
And heal
And it's real
– Salt defies false boundaries we've placed

I used to think healing
Was about putting things back together
And I would tune into a body
And see what was broken
The body would be white light
Except for where it wasn't
And where it wasn't was just needing light
I'd bring it and miracles happened
The miracles happened but they didn't always stick
Because the light wasn't meant to come from me
That was a quick fix
So then I learnt, it's not my job
But I can sure hold the space
And I would barely touch my friends from that point
I'd guide them into their own grace
And oh my goodness the shit that I witnessed
Bones healed
Muscles stitched back together
It never made sense to my medical mind
But actually the scientist in me was ever present
Because it makes total sense to become a vibration
And therefore to create an experience
And that's what they did every time and I'd witness
They become love and it was serious
A serious effect was had on the body
A serious change in the mind
Consciousness shifted and the 'not white' would go
A serious shift towards the light

Often I'd cry in awe as I'd see
Them realise their own power and they'd set their bodies free
– Sometimes you need someone to show you the salt path, but you have salt aplenty

Once upon a time
I was terrified
Of myself
Of my power
Of the natural world
And then
I realised I was a part of it
– Salt changed my life for the better

ELLIE ANN DEIGHTON

Once I realised salt was natural
The whole world opened
My nature opened
I no longer denied myself
I no longer made wrong who I am
And everything seemed like it would always be okay
– Salt made me realise everything and nothing matters and wow, it makes me light

I don't care if you tell me it's real or made up or delusional or insane
I care about the shift in my heart
And the magic that happens when the barrier between worlds collapses
And the way I feel so like myself in these conversations
And the curiosity we share in engaging in these conversations
And the peace that comes
And the peace that comes
And the peace that comes
– Salt guides me home (and can do the same for you)

…

Expansion.

Salt isn't simply a spiritual thing
Well, it depends on how you define it
But really, it's totally the way I live
How I sing my songs and write them
How I know how to build my altar
How I pull together lessons to teach
How I decide which car to bring home
It's how I choose—apricot or peach?
You bet in my life, when there's decisions
That need to be made, I'll be clear
It's salt that gets sprinkled all over the choice
And it slices through bullshit and fear
Suddenly I know the right call
Now I know it deeply, the vibration
And every time and when it makes no sense
Salt brings me to the perfect places
– Salt is more than ghost stories

It's my truth to buy a house
Salt says soon
Sugar says it has to look a certain way
Salt says you'll know it when you see it
Sugar says hurry up and stress about it
Salt says your house it out there, you'll find each other
Sugar says cancel everything else, you can only do so much
Salt says it all fits together
Sugar says now I've got it I must fill it
Salt says enjoy the space and fill it with inspiration
– Salt and sugar are very different

It's my calling to go to Scotland
Sugar says no, you can't do that
Salt says we're going to Scotland
Sugar says we'll go once this to-do list is complete
Salt says we're going in December
Sugar says I can't travel and work
Salt says yes and both
Sugar says don't enjoy it too much, it's rude to gloat
Salt says your best life is your highest service
Sugar says I'm too fat
Salt takes me to the place my body heals
– Salt knows better than sugar

It's my turn to do the food shop
Which doesn't happen often
It's not my strength or joy
But sometimes it's my responsibility
Sugar says panic, buy what's on special, have no plan
Salt asks my body what she wants
Sugar cares for price tags
Salt cares for alignment
Sugar over-purchases, over-compensates, under-nourishes
Salt calls my hands to pull foods into the basket
– One fills me, one fulfils me

When I accepted
That everything is a spiritual act
Every move is a ritual
I felt free
– I don't need to cast salt circles to be myself, I just need to be here

The Mystic Lived
The Epilogue

Salt told me to tell you...
Let me be clear,
Absolute.
Let me tell you
The truth
Let me say no
To you
Let me say yes
Despite you
Let me, I say
And really,
It's a nicety
I am not one for pleasing
I am one for truth
I am not one for seeking
A disguised version of you
I am here to be real
Unfiltered
Unprettied
I am here to heal the bruises
And I'm not here to pity.
I'm here, pleased to inform you
That when you let me in
Your life force will no longer be wasted
And your energy won't be thinned
For when you invite my lick into your life

You won't know the slipping of boundaries
When salt marries the blurs in your life with the answers
There won't be space for you off with fake fairies
Let me be clear,
Absolute.
Let me be clear
I'm here for the truth
If my *no* meets your *yes*
It might challenge you
If my *yes* hurts your *no*
You have work to do.
– A note from salt to you

I have been afraid of myself at times. Afraid of what might happen, what I might discover, should I sit in the dark and listen to myself. To really listen. I can recount time after time where I have sat in the ritual of listening to myself, of deeply attuning to my heart and I have received guidance from my true source that really scared me. I've had many of these sliding door moments where, within an instant of a truth becoming conscious, I have felt my concept of my world shatter, my concept of myself dissolve... and then... A moment of panic. A brief dissociation. I disappear from my own body until my next breath brings me back. It's not for long, just enough to jolt me, but I come right back in and then I see it.

The next step reveals itself like a trail of soft light showing me the way through the dark. The dark is my perception, what I think is going to happen and what I think I'm going to lose. The light is the truth. The light says, 'That's it, babe, this way. That's it, you can see me. That's it, one more step. That's it, you cast this spell. That's it, your dreams are coming true. Be brave now, it'll be better than expected...' And so I step forth. And so my life changes. And so my face shifts. And so my body is lighter. And so I remember a little more of who I am. This is the path of the mystic. We walk the unknown, often. It is misunderstood, even unto ourselves, but there is no question of whether it is worth it. The truth shows us the way if we are willing to listen to it, but only the true devotee will follow their light through the darkness and receive their dreams come true.

You can pick us from a crowd because our lives look different, feel different, taste different. We have a freedom about us you'll envy or admire or both. We have a way of being that allows us to pull the fabric of the universe as if we are knitting. You'll see life working out for us, catching us, again and again. You'll see love finding us again and again. You'll see friends chasing the world for us because of the way we love. You'll see people attack us, triggered by our owned sense of self, heck maybe you'll be one of the attackers. You will see a way of life that confounds you. We will know pain more intimately than you will imagine. Because you see the shiny parts. The lifestyle. The time freedom. The fans and friends. The shiny photoshoots. The pretty products. The wild productivity.

'Oh, she's written another book!' 'Oh, she's in love!' 'Oh, she's so fit!' And it won't be wild to you. Because it's us. The wild ones. We've done it again. Made more wild love out of life. But wild love isn't a secret thing passed onto only some of us. It is in the hands of us all. The truth is, the salt of it is, not all of us are willing to hold that wild love in our hands and live like our hearts damn well depend on it. Are you?

– Will you call forth the salt?

Will you call forth the salt?
Will you allow yourself the awakening granules that sting until you cry through them?
Will you express the weirdest part of you knowing it's the truest?
Will you allow your light to awaken your neighbour?
Will you wear the projections of all who don't yet understand as if they are simply rain clouds that soon too will pass?
Because you have to
You cannot hold onto those clouds
You cannot pretend your salt is a reason to hold extra water
Oh no
Your salt is the reason to keep things perfectly hydrated
Keep your skin plump
Keep your life bountiful
But don't flood yourself with unnecessary pressures
And don't kid yourself with trying to fix the stubborn
Let your gifts dance with the willing
Let it be that we each live our path
Let it be known that your only job is to stick to yours
– Only you can call your salt forth and stick with it

earth roots sing

out nov 2025

A touch of EARTH

Earth hums
She is a present underfoot
A tone we lay upon
A frequency we dance to
Earth is where we return
Over and over and over in our life
And of course, in the end
Earth is where we go
Where the dust goes and settles
Where the ashes go and rest
But what never ends
Is her song
And the way her roots reach down
Touching every one of us along the way
– Earth roots sing
Not all earth is silent
Read *Earth Roots Sing* now CLICK HERE

ELLIE ANN DEIGHTON

Earth is calling. Will you answer?
Read **_Earth Roots Sing_** Now

About the author

She teaches humans how to live in the light of their true selves and she goes first.

Like an integrity radar

Through life

Hers and yours

She will find the cracks

And spit them out

Until your world tastes like honey together

For she is not here to walk alone

And neither are you.

It is no mistake that you are here reading this.

Is it stories in her books calling you in for a journey?

Is her music singing you home to the temple of you?

Is her curriculum asking you to become more of yourself?

Is now the time?

I believe so.

The scientist in her has a hypothesis,

That you are magic,

The facilitator in her

Can prove it,

The witch in her
Can give you the tools to cast it,
The woman in her
Can celebrate you as you shine,
The artist in her
Is on stage creating beside you.
You are magic,
And here,
You will find that you are home.
– about Ellie, author of **Salt Sugar Spirit**

Author's note

You will never be alone

For you will always have your salt

And magic will always be inside you

Beckoning your return to your guiding heart

You can close your eyes and see the sparkles

And you can open your eyes and look for the sprinkles

And you can place your hands on your body and feel the boundaries

And you can move your body and hear the salt whisper

And even on the darkest days

There can be a light

Because of your willingness to be with your salt

And the greatest gift you could ever give yourself

Is to learn to

See

Listen

Feel

Receive

Remember

Play

Speak

Be

Salt

And let the extrasensory part of you be
– Salt is what I teach

And I can teach you to be one with your salt too
Or you can receive little pinches of salt to your inbox
Subscribe for bonuses at elliedeighton.com/salt

Extrasensory: School of Light
An Invitation & Self Enquiry

Are you scared of Extrasensory School?
Because there's no doubt about it,
Waking up is scary.
Waking up is to realise the areas in your life that are out of alignment,
That are not serving you on your highest path,
That are not supporting your fulfilment of your spirit's mission,
And that can be unsettling.
It's true.
I remember waking up to the reality that becoming a surgeon wasn't my highest expression.
It shook me.
It threw me.
It cost me relationships, friendships I thought I'd keep for a lifetime.
I've learnt that I can keep holding onto my limitations or I can be myself
And I cannot have both.
I will always as a human have limitations of course,
But that's different to holding on and pouring energy into them.

I freed myself the day I said, 'I will choose my heart no matter what,'
And I wish I'd had support in that earlier.
I wished back then to not walk that path alone...
But once I wished for aligned support it arrived.
If you're afraid of Extrasensory School that's okay, in fact it's not the best question to ask.
The best is: Would this be aligned support for you in your spiritual path and mission?
That's the question that matters.
That's the question that should have you clicking the button to book a call with my team if the answer is yes.
I'll see you in the journey
– **Extrasensory** is the salt-led path

Join Ellie in **Extrasensory: School of Light**, an online group pilgrimage into the realm of salt and spiritual awakening.

Use the discount code SALTORSUGAR to begin your journey today.
https://www.thegeniusportal.com.au/extrasensory

Acknowledgements

Clare

Mem

William

Paige

Elissa

Chris

Timothy

Urs

Joseph

Leah

Kel

Luke

Elise

Elijah

Noah

Daphne

Anthony

Peggy

Dock

Ann

Tony
Donelle
Robert
Nadia
Jodie
Celeste
Adelle
Rachel
Rachael
Rebekah
Tom

– Thank you for revealing your salt to me, **Salt Sugar Spirit** wouldn't exist without you.

www.ingramcontent.com/pod-product-compliance
Lightning Source LLC
Chambersburg PA
CBHW071245070526
44583CB00017B/2334